A fashionable HISTORY of DRESSES & SKIRTS

Raintree

A FASHIONABLE HISTORY OF DRESSES &
SKIRTS
was produced by

David West ☆☆ Children's Books
7 Princeton Court
55 Felsham Road
London SW15 1AZ

This edition first published in the United States in
2003 by Raintree, a division of Reed Elsevier, Inc.,
Chicago, Illinois.

For information address the publisher:
Raintree
100 N. LaSalle
Suite 1200
Chicago, IL 60602

Author: Helen Reynolds
Editors: Clare Hibbert, Marta Segal Block
Picture Research: Carlotta Cooper
Designer: Julie Joubinaux

Library of Congress Cataloging-in-Publication Data:
Reynolds, Helen, 1956-
  Dresses and skirts / Helen Reynolds.
    p. cm. -- (A fashionable history of costume)
Summary: A look at changing trends of fashion throughout history,
with
an emphasis on dresses and skirts.
Includes bibliographical references and index.
  ISBN 1-4109-0031-2 (lib. bdg.)
  1. Dresses--Juvenile literature. 2. Skirts--Juvenile literature. [1.
Dresses. 2. Skirts. 3. Fashion--History.] I. Title. II. Series.
  GT2060.R49 2003
  391.4--dc21
                                2002153953

ISBN 1-4109-0031-2

07 06 05 04 03
10 9 8 7 6 5 4 3 2 1

PHOTO CREDITS:

Abbreviations: t-top, m-middle, b-bottom, r-right,
l-left, c-center.

The publisher would like to thank the following
for permission to reproduce photographs: Front
cover m & 19br – Rex Features Ltd; front cover tl,
3 & 12bl – Dover Books; front cover r & 14l –
Mary Evans Picture Library; pages 4tr, 7tr, 9br,
12mr, 21tr, 25br – The Culture Archive; pages 4-
5b, 6-7, 7m, 18br, 22tr & br, 26tr – Dover Books;
pages 5bm & 21l, 5br, 11tr, 13br, 15 all, 17 both,
19b, 21br, 22bl, 22-23, 23r, 26tl, 27br, 29tl – Rex
Features Ltd; pages 6tr & bl, 8tr & br, 8-9, 9tr,
10tr, 12tl, 13tl, 16tr, 16-17, 18tl, 20tl, 20-21, 24bl,
24-25b, 25tr, 26bl, 27l, 28 both – Mary Evans
Picture Library; page 7br – Digital Stock; pages
10bl, 11ml, 14mr, 16bl – Hulton Archive; page
11bl – Irving Solero/The Museum at the Fashion
Institute of Technology; page 13bm – Karen
Augusta, www.antique-fashion.com; page 19l –
V&A Picture Library; page 24tl - © National Trust
Photographic Library/Derrick E. Witty; pages 28-
29b – Corbis Images; pages 29tr & br – Katz/FSP.

Printed and bound in China

A *fashionable* HISTORY of DRESSES & SKIRTS

Contents

Making a deerskin dress

Native Americans hunted animals for food, then made full use of their kill, stitching soft, warm clothes from the skins.

Greek tunic

Dresses in ancient times involved little sewing. This 19th century copy of a Greek tunic, or chiton, is pinned at the shoulders and belted at the waist.

From Skins to Spandex

The very first dresses and skirts were probably the animal skins worn by the earliest humans. Later, people learned to make cloth, which both men and women draped around their bodies. At first, great care was taken so that cloth wasn't wasted. This became less important as cloth-making techniques improved. Women's clothes became more elaborate—and uncomfortable. Because wealthy women generally stayed home and did not need much freedom of movement, clothes that were beautiful but uncomfortable were acceptable.

Then, in the 20th century, as more women began to lead more active lives, they wanted clothes that were more practical.

Advances in human-made fabrics have helped create clothes that are simple and comfortable, but still stylish.

DESIGNER EVENING GOWN

Designer dresses like this one, worn by the actress Halle Berry, are made from exquisite, expensive fabrics. They are cut to fit the body of the wearer exactly.

PVC MINI DRESS

PVC, a type of thin vinyl, is an example of human-made materials that has been used in fashion.

Wrapping

The first dresses and skirts were lengths of cloth wrapped around the body. As people became more interested in fashion, the cloth was draped, folded, pleated, tucked, and knotted. Clothing showed off both the body and the fabric. The ancient Egyptians, Persians, Greeks, and Romans all wrapped their clothes around their bodies.

Classical cloaks

Ancient civilizations turned wrapping into an art form. The Greek cloak, or himation, was a large rectangle of cloth wrapped around the body and pinned at the shoulder with a brooch. The Roman toga was made from an enormous half circle of material. It was worn over a tunic and wound around the body so that it fell in complex folds.

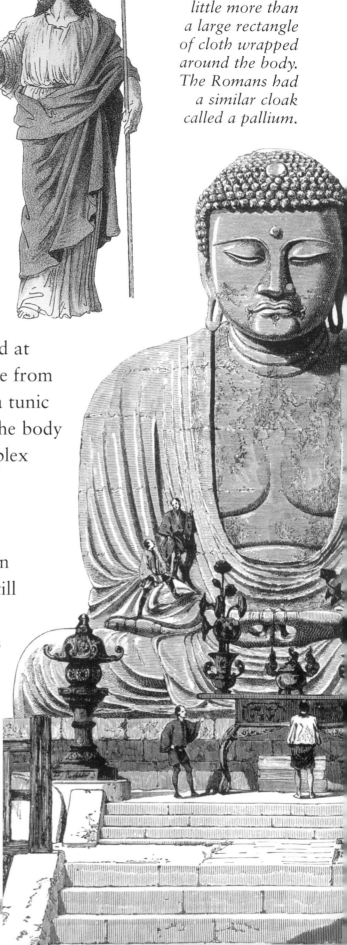

GREEK CLOAK

The himation was little more than a large rectangle of cloth wrapped around the body. The Romans had a similar cloak called a pallium.

Keeping warm

Long after the Roman Empire fell, people still created clothes by wrapping—but styles were simpler. The Saxons, Danes, and Celts wrapped extra layers of cloth around the body to keep warm. These cloaks, or mantles, were worn until the Middle Ages.

ROMAN TOGAS

Roman men wore outer garments called togas on special occasions. Ordinary citizens wore white ones. The Roman emperor's toga was a rich purple, colored with expensive dyes.

Design on the stand

The ancient art of wrapping is used in fashionable dressmaking. Designers wrap material around a tailor's dummy, or stand, then cut and pin the pieces back together to create the garment's shape. Next, the design on the stand is taken apart so a paper pattern can be made. Today computers are often used to help in this process.

"Design on the stand" reached its peak in the 1930s—a time of flowing, draped dresses. A master of this method was the French couturier Alix Grès (1903–93), who originally trained as a sculptor. Her imaginative, Greek-style evening gowns were cleverly wrapped and draped to create beautiful, asymmetric (irregular) shapes.

A Grès creation

Grès favored soft, fluid fabrics such as jersey and silk. These complemented her draping technique.

The versatile sari

The traditional dress of Indian women is the sari, a long length of cotton or silk that wraps around the body.

Set in stone

Stonecarvers created this statue of the Buddha long ago. But Buddhist monks today still wear similar flowing robes.

Beating the heat

In hot countries, a simple wraparound cloth is cool and comfortable.

The Tunic

The tunic is one of the simplest forms of dress. The Greeks and Romans wore it, tied around the waist with a cord, or girdle. Over the centuries tunics have continued to be a wardrobe staple. They are versatile garments, easily adaptable to both elaborate and simple fashions.

Clothing for all classes

In Great Britain, the tunic changed little from the time of Roman rule (43–400 C.E.) up to the Norman Conquest (1066), when troops from Northern France took control. The tunic was worn by everyone—serfs, yeoman farmers, and the nobility. It was even worn by soldiers as a surcoat (outer garment) over their chain mail. Tunics remained the basic dress for both men and women until the 1300s. Then, people dropped the tunic for more complex garment styles.

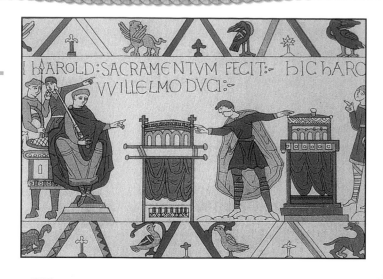

THE BAYEUX TAPESTRY
Medieval tapestries like this one can provide us with information about what people wore in those days. This tapestry is probably from the 11th Century.

KNIGHTS HOSPITALLERS
These medieval knights wore a tunic and cloak even when dressed for battle. The Hospitallers took part in the Crusades, but they also cared for the sick.

The haute couture tunic

At the beginning of the 20th century, the basic tunic shape came back into fashion. French couturier Paul Poiret (1879–1944) drew inspiration from Asian tunics. His collections featured baggy harem pants worn under lampshade tunics, so-called because they were wired at the bottom to stand out in a circle around the body. Poiret's striking clothes were made from rich, exotic fabrics, such as silks, brocades, and velvets.

Sixties style

The tunic mini dress was the height of fashion during the 1960s. Women teamed short tunics with form-fitting sweaters or blouses.

Made from the latest synthetic fabrics, such as polyester and nylon, tunic mini dresses had a stiff, strong silhouette.

RUSSIAN PEASANT DRESS

Until World War I, Russian women wore simple, belted tunics like these. The tunic remains an important part of traditional dress in many countries.

SCHOOL TUNICS

During the 1920s and 1930s, schoolgirls wore box-pleated tunics over a blouse and tie. Tunics were made in sensible, dark gabardine—a durable wool and cotton mix that did not show dirt.

The Tailored Dress

In Europe in the Middle Ages, the cut of women's dresses became more sophisticated. Tailors put in seams to give garments more shape. At first, fashionable dresses followed the natural contours of the body—later on, women would be molding their bodies to fit the clothes!

Fit for a princess

In the second half of the 19th century, a dress style was introduced that was shaped without a waist seam. It fitted tightly around the bust, and had an extra piece of fabric, or gore, sewn in so that it flared out over the bustle. Cut in panels from shoulder to hem, this style was named the princess dress in honor of Alexandra, Princess of Wales (1844–1925). A variation was the princess polonaise, in which the skirt was drawn up at the back to reveal a frilly underskirt.

Noblewoman's Gown
High ranking ladies of the 1300s wore dresses with trains. Over the tunic is an unbelted over-gown, tailored in at the waist. The long, streamer sleeves were called tippets.

New shapes

In the 1950s dresses made in unusual shapes became popular. The trapeze line dress had sides that slanted outward like a trapezoid. The A-line was very similar, but was shaped like the letter "A." Introduced in 1955 by Christian Dior (1905–1957), this flattering shape has since been used by many designers.

Princess Alexandra and her Daughters
Alexandra married Britain's future King Edward VII in 1863. She is pictured here with their daughters Louise, Victoria, and Maud. In this photograph they are all wearing princess dresses.

Vionnet Outfit

Below: This 1920s dress and matching cape demonstrate Madeleine Vionnet's clever, flowing lines. A snug-fitting hat and beaded purse complete the look.

Long & Lean Eveningwear

Above: In the 1930s, women wore romantic, floor-sweeping evening gowns like these that showed off their curves. On top they wore a short jacket with padded shoulders.

A cut above

One 20th-century designer who made dresses that adapted to the wearer's body (rather than the other way around) was Madeleine Vionnet (1876–1975). She achieved her fit with unusual seaming. Since Vionnet clothes were bias-cut (cut diagonally across the grain of the cloth), they seemed limp and shapeless—until they were put on! Then they transformed into smooth, fluid dresses. Not as famous as her contemporaries Coco Chanel (1883–1971) and Elsa Schiaparelli (1890–1973), Vionnet is still regarded as the master of the dress and its construction.

A-line Woolen Mini Dress

This example of an A-line dress clearly shows the sharp angles that were popular in the dresses of the 1950s and 1960s.

The Waist

Fashion is constantly changing. One of the most striking changes in the shape of European women's dress came during the Renaissance. Women's waists gained more prominence as the loose, belted medieval dress was replaced by a fitted bodice, worn over a gathered skirt.

Waist watchers!

The Renaissance was a time of great wealth. In England, the Tudor dynasty held the throne and trade flourished. Beautiful cloths were produced, including sumptuous velvets and elaborate silk brocades.

These fabrics were heavy, stiff, and totally unsuitable for the flowing gowns that had been fashionable in medieval times. Instead, tailors used them to create more structured styles that emphasized the waist.

In the following centuries the waist position fluctuated but always remained defined. The waist reached its highest point around 1800 with the empire, or directoire, style. The look was inspired by the flowing robes of ancient Roman dress.

WORTH GOWN
Crinolines and bustles were made popular by Charles Frederick Worth (1825–1895). He dressed all the most fashionable ladies in Paris.

ELIZABETHAN DRESS
Only a wealthy woman could have owned this 1853 dress. The bodice and skirt are in rich brocade; the ruff and cuffs are in expensive lace.

DIRECTOIRE OR EMPIRE DRESS
The fine, gauzy dresses popular during the Directoire period had high waists that began just below the bust. This look was made popular by the Empress Joséphine (1763–1814), first wife of Napoleon Bonaparte (1769–1821).

High, low, or somewhere in the middle
Dress styles returned the waist to its proper place around 1850. Waists were accentuated by immensely wide skirts, supported on a cage of crinoline. In the 1900s, waists rose in a classical revival, then in the 1920s they fell to hip level with flapper fashions.

Following World War II (1939–1945), Christian Dior introduced his New Look in 1947. Romantic and glamorous, the style emphasized the waist with big, billowing skirts.

A DRESS TO DANCE IN
Flappers were the fashionable young women of the 1920s, known for their shockingly short haircuts—and skirts! With its low waist and fringed hem, this dress gave a flapper perfect freedom to enjoy the latest energetic dances, such as the Charleston.

DIOR'S NEW LOOK
In 1947, Christian Dior created the New Look, which really drew attention to the waist. After the rationing of World War II, this look was an instant sensation—the skirts used extravagant quantities of fabric!

The Working Wardrobe

The vast crinolines of the Victorian era restricted women's movement. Two women who argued for more practical women's dress were Amelia Bloomer (1818–1894) and Elizabeth Cady Stanton (1815–1902). These early feminists promoted the bloomer outfit—a knee-length, loose dress worn over baggy trousers (bloomers). Unfortunately, most people viewed the style as a joke.

Wool suit

By the late 19th century, more and more women were working in offices. The most practical outfit was a suit, such as this trim, tailored jacket and skirt.

Shortages

During World War II, labor and fabric were scarce. Clothing was designed to be practical and durable. Manufacturers followed strict rules to avoid wasting any cloth.

Suits make sense

As more women began to work outside of the home, women's clothes were made more practical. By the late 1800s an increasing number of women were working in offices. They needed outfits that looked good, but were also easy to wear and care for. "Separates" made perfect fashion sense. By the end of the 1800s, women had adapted the man's jacket, wearing it over a blouse with a matching skirt. This became their working wardrobe. Today the suit remains the professional woman's key outfit, though its exact style changes almost every season.

CHANEL TWEED SUIT

Karl Lagerfeld (1938–) became design director at Chanel in 1983. This is one of his versions of the classic, boxy suits that made Coco Chanel famous.

POWER SUIT

Power dressing was a term used in the 1980s to describe the suits worn by businesswomen. Although this one has the typical boxy shape, padded shoulders, and short skirt, its fabric and hat mean it is clearly only for the fashion runway.

PAUL SMITH SUIT

British designer Paul Smith (1946–) gained a reputation for suiting up some of the world's movers and shakers early in the 21st century. Here is an example of one of his modern suits.

15

Straight & Narrow

From the 15th century, when the flowing medieval gown gradually disappeared, until the 19th century, most "dresses" were in fact separates—bodices worn with a skirt and petticoat. During the 19th century, it became fashionable to wear a skirt in a heavier fabric with a lighter bodice or blouse. This was the beginning of the modern skirt.

The search for a wearable skirt

In the early 20th century, designers looked at ways to make the skirt more comfortable. One ill-fated design was Paul Poiret's hobble skirt of 1911. It was comfortably loose at the hips, but so tight at the ankle that walking was almost impossible. The hobble was shortlived, but caused quite a stir.

After World War I, Jean Patou (1880–1936) and Coco Chanel began to make sporty clothes for active women. Stopping at the calf or knee, skirts often had pleats for easy movement.

THE LATEST SACK-RACE

Donald McGill

Poking fun at the hobble

It was hard to move quickly in the hobble skirt because it was so tight around the calves. Wearers could only take very small steps—or jumps! Contemporary cartoonists had a field day.

Adapting the hobble

In this 1914 picture, London society gathers for a cricket match. Here the hobble skirt has already been redesigned The draped slit at the front frees the legs, so walking is easier.

Jersey suits in the styles of Chanel & Patou

Shorter, sportier skirts came into fashion in the 1920s. They were worn with loose, knitted cardigans or jackets.

Pencil skirt, 1950s

Because it used little fabric, the knee-length straight skirt was very popular in the wartime 1940s. In the 1950s the style lengthened and became known as the pencil skirt. It was usually teamed with a short, shaped jacket.

Sleek & chic

Throughout the 1920s the designer Coco Chanel made clothes that were comfortable, practical, and sporty. Her loose cardigans and twinsets (two sweaters worn together) were teamed with straight, knee-length skirts. Although Chanel's designs were high fashion, their simple shape made them easy to copy. They quickly filtered down to the mass market.

Long, straight pencil skirts became particularly fashionable in the 1950s. Cheap to produce, they looked elegant when worn with a jacket and high heels. Modeled by the most beautiful trendsetters of the day, pencil skirts were popular with women of all ages. Teamed with the latest, figure-hugging sweaters, they were especially popular with younger women.

Hobbled again!

In the 1990s, the long, slim hobble skirt returned. This time around clever cutting, slits, or modern, stretchy Lycra made it far easier to walk in.

Popular Pleats

Pleats are folds of fabric that provide fullness in dresses and skirts. They can do this in different ways. During the 18th century, loose-fitting sack dresses featured deep box pleats running down the back, from the neck to the hem. Later, the width of a 19th-century crinoline came from rows and rows of neat pleats at the waistline. Pleats are also used on skirts for decoration.

Egyptian pleats

The ancient Egyptians made beautiful, pleated clothing from linen, a light cloth. Around 3,500 years ago, the cloaks, skirts, and dresses worn by the Egyptian royalty and nobility were decorated with rows of fine pleats.

Victorian pleats

The Victorians loved decoration. Small pin pleats decorated their cotton blouses. Clothing designed to be worn for sports, such as bicycling, tennis, or gymnastics, had roomy pleats to allow for ease of movement.

EVIDENCE OF EGYPTIAN PLEATS

Only a few scraps of linen dresses from ancient Egypt survive. But clothing in the many Egyptian wallpaintings and statues is often intricately pleated.

VICTORIAN SCHOOLGIRL DRESSED FOR THE GYM

In Britain, going to school became compulsory in the 1800s. New schools were built, all with gymnasiums. Physical education was an important part of the day at schools for both girls and boys.

Pleats are here to stay

Spanish-born designer Mariano Fortuny (1871–1949) patented his own special method of pleating in 1909. He used it to create his Delphos dress, a flowing gown made of tightly pleated silk or velvet. This dress is a design classic.

In the 1950s, chemists came up with ways to treat material so that pleats stayed in permanently, without ironing. "Swish" skirts designed for dancing to the rock and roll music of the day often featured accordion and sunray pleats.

FORTUNY'S DELPHOS DRESS OF 1920

Fortuny's clever pleating makes silk catch the light beautifully.

PERMANENT PLEATS

In this wool dress designed in 1955, pressed pleats radiate out from the hip seam.

ROCKERS REUNION

These rock and roll fans of the 1980s are wearing pleated skirts that were first popular in the 1950s.

A Glimpse of Flesh

One of the reasons we wear clothes is to look good. However, what looks beautiful to one generation or culture may appear ugly to the next. In different times we have covered certain parts of our body while leaving others exposed. What we choose to expose depends on the fashions and values of our culture.

A hint of cleavage

Excavations on the Greek island of Crete show that Minoan women may have worn elaborate, fitted dresses that exposed the breasts. Such a style is unusual—dresses from earliest times have always modestly covered the breasts.

Low necklines that daringly reveal some cleavage have come in and out of fashion. In the 19th century, the respectable woman was always well covered. However, Charles Frederick Worth's extravagant designs included some racy evening wear that had extremely low, or décolleté, necklines.

COURT DRESS

Low, square-cut bodices were fashionable in the 16th century. The stiff, tight-fitting fabric showed off women's cleavages.

CAMILLE CLIFFORD, THE GIBSON GIRL

Actress Camille Clifford (1885–1971) poses with her hair piled high to reveal a long neck, bare shoulders, and an hourglass figure. She was one of the Gibson Girls, drawn by artist Charles Gibson (1867–1944). His pen-and-ink drawings captured many fashionable women of the day.

Minis, Midis & Maxis

Unless you had very thin legs, the miniskirt was a difficult fashion to wear. In the late 1960s, midis and maxis came along, giving women the option of exposing far less leg.

Less is more!

In the 20th century, low necklines were not very common, although 1930s evening gowns often had low backs. In the 1960s a revolution occurred when Mary Quant (1934-) popularized the miniskirt, which revealed more leg than ever before. Since then, designers have shown just about every body part, including the bare midriff. There have even been crazes for slashed, peephole clothes.

Sixties see-through

This mini dress is made from semitransparent plastic!

Hipster comeback

This outfit of 2002 is by Spanish-born designer Amaya Arzuaga (1971–). The low waistline and tiny top reveal a lot of bare flesh.

World Fashions

When different cultures meet, ideas about fashion tend to get exchanged. For Europeans, the East has always been a source of fabrics and ideas. The Silk Road, originally used by ancient Roman traders to carry silks from China, was reopened in the 1400s.

East meets West

In the 1600s, Indian textiles becme popular, thanks to trade fostered by the East India Company (1600–1708). In the late 1800s, department stores like Liberty in London and R.H. Macy & Co. in New York sold fabrics from all over the world: cashmere from Persia (now Iran), crepe from Japan, and silk from China and India.

Kimonos from Japan

A pure silk kimono is still the traditional choice for Japanese women when attending special ceremonies. It is worn with an obi, a broad sash, that ties in an elaborate bow. In the West, the kimono inspired the boudoir gowns of the early 1900s and the dressing gowns of the 1920s.

The Laura Ashley Look

Above: Designer Laura Ashley (1925–1985) was well known for her romantic "peasant-inspired" looks, like this dress from 1970.

Japanese design today

Since the 1970s, Japanese designers have found worldwide success. Like many of his contemporaries, Kansai Yamamoto (1944–) learned how to structure his clothes by looking at traditional Japanese dress. Mixing in modern details, Yamamoto creates elegant dresses in a clean, uncluttered style (right).

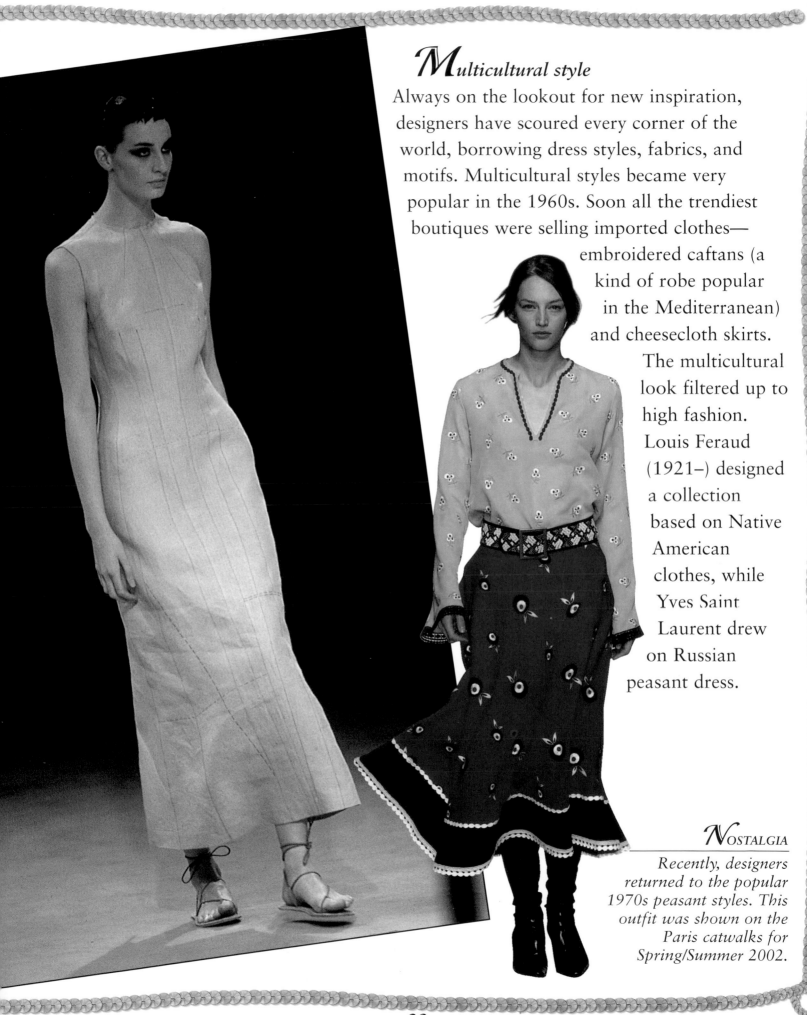

Multicultural style

Always on the lookout for new inspiration, designers have scoured every corner of the world, borrowing dress styles, fabrics, and motifs. Multicultural styles became very popular in the 1960s. Soon all the trendiest boutiques were selling imported clothes—embroidered caftans (a kind of robe popular in the Mediterranean) and cheesecloth skirts.

The multicultural look filtered up to high fashion. Louis Feraud (1921–) designed a collection based on Native American clothes, while Yves Saint Laurent drew on Russian peasant dress.

Nostalgia

Recently, designers returned to the popular 1970s peasant styles. This outfit was shown on the Paris catwalks for Spring/Summer 2002.

Children's Dresses

C̶hildren's clothing reflects the societies they live in. Until the end of the 18th century, babies and very young children were dressed in long gowns worn over swaddling clothes. Swaddling clothes were like bandages which wrapped up the baby, protecting its arms and legs. Once free of these clothes, girls were put into restrictive dresses that were miniature copies of the ones worn by their mothers.

Modest movement

At the beginning of the 19th century, fashions were changing. Girls began to wear less awkward dresses, but modesty was still very important. Pantalets (long underwear) were worn under dresses. Trimmed with pretty pin tucks or lace, pantalets reached the ankles. This meant a girl could raise her skirts for easier movement —without offending anyone by exposing her leg.

In the 1600s boys wore dresses until they were breeched—put in a pair of breeches (pants). As the centuries passed, breeching took place earlier and earlier until gowns were reserved for baby girls.

T̶RADITIONAL CHRISTENING ROBE, 1863

Left: Traditionally long white robes were worn by baby boys and girls for their christening. Made in fine laces and embroidery, such robes often became family heirlooms, handed down through the generations.

24

Frills & flounces

The Victorians adored frills and flounces. Compared to the mass-produced clothes of today, Victorian children's wear was expensive. For this reason, clothes had deep tucks, big hems, and wide seams so that they could be altered to fit as the child grew.

When playing, girls often wore pinafores or smocks to protect their dresses. The smock was based on garments worn by farm workers over their clothes. It was gathered at the top, or yoke, and had puffed sleeves. Usually home-sewn, it often had decorative embroidery.

VICTORIAN GIRL IN PANTALETS

Girls' dresses were full like their mothers' but shorter for easier movement. Pretty pantalets were worn underneath to keep the legs modestly covered.

Child-friendly

In the 20th century, companies began to specialize in children's wear, but styles remained easier-to-wear versions of adult fashions. Prices came down thanks to mass production. From the 1950s, the sportier adult styles crossed over into children's dress, resulting in more comfortable clothes. Around this period, designers saw the potential of the teen market. Stores opened that sold clothes designed just for teenagers.

FRENCH CHILDRENSWEAR

In the 1930s, girls' dresses followed the same curvy lines as adult women's clothes.

SWEET SMOCK

This children's book illustration shows a typical toddler's smock of the mid-20th century.

Men in Skirts

We usually think of the skirt as a garment for women, but men have long worn skirts—from simple grass skirts to pleated kilts. Skirts for men are part of the traditional national dress in a number of countries. The white, pleated fustanella is still part of the uniform of the Greek national guard, worn for special occasions.

Cool Linen

High-ranking ancient Egyptian men wore wrapped skirts that were sometimes pleated. Made of fine linen, these wrapped skirts would have been comfortably cool in the Egyptian heat.

The Fustanella

This white, pleated kilt remains the national dress for Greek and Albanian men. Its name comes from fustian, the coarse cotton cloth used to make it.

The kilt

One of the best-known men's skirts is the tartan kilt. Tartan is a checked, woolen cloth made in Scotland. It is believed the cloth may date back to the 1400s, and today there are more than 1,300 known styles. Each clan, or family, has its own tartan with its own coloring and style of check. The kilt is now part of Scotland's national dress, worn worldwide by people of Scottish ancestry.

Since the 1980s the kilt has reemerged as a sign of national pride. It is especially popular among young Scottish soccer fans.

Whirling Skirts

The Islamic whirling dervishes (founded in 1273) are famed for their wild dancing. Spinning in swirling skirts, they enter a trance which, they hope, will bring them closer to Allah.

HIGHLAND DRESS, C.1902

It takes over 7 1/2 yards of cloth to make the traditional kilt, which is worn with a matching length of plaid that pins at the shoulder. A fur pouch called a sporran hangs from the belt in the front.

Men's skirts in haute couture

Today skirts for men can be high fashion. Jean-Paul Gaultier (1952–), known for his witty designs, has included kilts in his men's wear collections. Few men except those paid to model his short and showy skirts wear them. However, haute couture fashions often show up on real people a few years later. It's hard to say what we may see soon.

JEAN-PAUL GAULTIER KILT

Gaultier's designs often shock! This pleated mini is his fun update of the kilt.

Fashionable Technology

Until the 1800s all garments were hand-sewn, either by tailors or by people in their homes. The sewing machine revolutionized the business of making clothing. Clothing could be put together more quickly, cheaply, and easily than ever before.

Birth of the sewing machine

Starting in the late 1700s, various inventors tried to design a machine that could mimic hand-stitching. This was finally achieved by an American, Elias Howe (1819–1867). He patented his sewing machine in 1846. Millions of machines sold worldwide. Factories equipped with sewing machines could turn out garments at high speed. As production rose, prices fell, and fashion became more affordable for everyone.

MASTER TAILOR OF THE 1640s

Cutting clothes that hang well requires skill. In the past, young tailors served as unpaid apprentices while learning their craft.

THE FIRST SEWING MACHINE

Elias Howe unveiled his machine in 1845. It made 200 stitches a minute—seven times as fast as any sewer! Along with the invention of the paper dress pattern, the sewing machine made home dressmaking far easier.

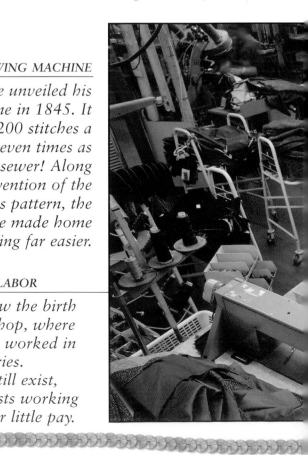

SWEATSHOP LABOR

The 1800s saw the birth of the sweatshop, where many women worked in terrible factories. Sweatshops still exist, with machinists working long hours for little pay.

Fabulous new fabrics

The creation of human-made materials also had a large impact on clothing. The first was rayon. It looked like silk or satin, but was much cheaper to produce. It was first used for flapper dresses in the early 1900s.

Synthetic materials, such as nylon and polyester, have other advantages besides low cost. They tend not to crease like cotton or silk, and unlike wool, they hold their shape well. Mixing them with natural fibers produces materials that keep the best aspects of both, a garment that holds its shape while still being comfortable and affordable.

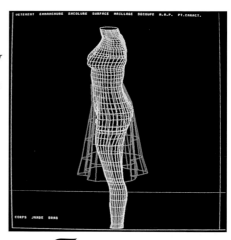

THE COMPUTER AGE

Computers are a great design tool. They can show how a finished dress will look, and even create an exact pattern for the cutters to follow.

PLATED METAL BY PACO RABANNE

Spanish-born Rabanne (1934–) is famous for making dresses out of highly unusual materials, such as metal, paper, and plastics.

JOHN GALLIANO AT WORK

Traditional dressmaking techniques live on in the world of high fashion. Unlike mass-produced clothes, designer dresses and skirts are handmade to order for a perfect, flattering fit.

Timeline

Prehistory
The first garments were animal skins and later, woven cloth wrapped around the body.

The ancient world
The ancient Egyptians, Greeks, and Romans all wore highly stylized versions of the tunic and wrap.

The Middle Ages
Tunics were simplified and long sleeves were added. By the 1400s, the dress was shaped to fit the body. Waist girdles accentuated the natural waist. The fashionable neckline lowered and sleeves were long and flowing.

16th century
The fashionable dress had a structured shape and was made in heavy silks and velvets. Bodices were stiff and long, ending in a "V" at the front. The bell-shaped skirt was left open in front to reveal the petticoat. In the second half of the century, ruffs made of starched materials became popular. Ruffs could encircle the neck or be left open. Dresses had enormous, billowing sleeves and skirts were supported by the farthingale (a hooped underskirt made of whalebone).

17th century
Lighter fabrics were in fashion so farthingales were no longer necessary. Waistlines rose. The ruff was replaced with collars of linen and lace. Sleeves ended at the elbow with lace cuffs.

18th century
The fashionable woman began to wear a hoop under her skirts. Skirts were again made of rich, heavy fabrics. The hoop was later replaced with a pannier (hoop) on each side of the hips, making dresses wide and narrow. Then, while heavy brocades remained popular at the royal court, fashionable society wore dresses made from light, hand-painted silks, muslins, and lawns. While the necklines of evening gowns were revealing, day dresses were often worn with a kerchief to cover the bare neck. The loose-fitting sack gown, which had box pleats falling down the back, was worn at home. At the end of the century, hoops disappeared as dresses became more reminiscent of classical times.

19th century
At the beginning of the century, high-waisted classical dresses remained fashionable. Long, slim evening gowns had low, square necklines and short, puffed sleeves. As the century progressed, the line of the waist dropped and so did the sleeve seam, resulting in sloping shoulders. By 1850, the numerous heavy petticoats were replaced by the crinoline cage—resulting in skirts of enormous widths. Within a decade the fullness moved to the back with the introduction of the crinolette and, later, the bustle. Toward the end of the century, fashionable women wore the S-line dress. Blouses, fitted jackets, and long skirts were popular.

20th century & beyond
Campaigns by dress reformers led to more comfortable fashions. By the 1920s, hems had risen to the knee. The waistline also dropped, creating a shape that hid the bust and hips. The 1930s saw the return of feminine curves, and the backless evening gown was popular. In 1947 the New Look was introduced with its small waists and billowing skirts. In the 1960s, the mini dress came in. Long, peasant skirts were popular in the 1970s. The next decade saw the business woman in "power suits," with a short, slim skirt. Evening wear was romantic, with full skirts. In the 1990s, and at the start of the 21st century, the emphasis was on individual style. Skirts could be full or slim, sweeping the floor or barely covering underwear!

*G*lossary

bodice upper portion of a dress, generally attached to the skirt at the waist

brocade heavy, often expensive fabric decorated with raised designs

bustle padding worn under the skirt to push it out at the back. Bustle skirts were in fashion during the 1860s and 1870s.

catwalk narrow walkway on which models parade clothing during fashion shows, also called a runway

couturier person who designs fashionable, custom-made clothing

crepe fabric, especially silk, that has been heat-treated to create a crinkled texture

crinoline stiff fabric held up by a frame of hoops made of whalebone or steel. Crinolines were used from the 1850s to hold out enormously wide skirts.

gabardine dense fabric that has a fine diagonal rib effect, popular for suits, coats, and skirts

girdle cord that encircles the waist. It was used as a belt for the medieval tunic dress.

gore dressmaking method to create fullness without the use of pleats or gathers. Gored skirts have a sewn-in panel, producing a close fit at the waist and a flared hem.

haute couture French for "high dressmaking." These garments are constructed to the client's personal measurements. The workmanship of haute couture is usually superb.

himation rectangular garment worn by the Ancient Greeks

kilt a knee-length, pleated skirt, made of a type of plaid wool called tartan, traditionally worn by Scottish men

pleat fold in cloth

sari traditional garment of women in India, consisting of a length of silk draped over one shoulder and wrapped around the body

sarong long, wrapped skirt worn by both men and women in many warmer climates, especially Malaysia

smocking decorative stitches to hold in fullness. First used on laborers' smocks, it decorated the yoke of children's dresses from the 19th century onwards.

tunic simple, loose-fitting garment such as those worn by the ancient Greeks and Romans, usually knee-length or longer and belted at the waist

twinset two sweaters made to be worn together, one sweater is a pullover, the other a cardigan

Index